GHOSTS
IN THE GARDEN

OTHER BOOKS BY BETH KEPHART

A Slant of Sun: One Child's Courage (Norton, 1998)

*Into the Tangle of Friendship: A Memoir of the Things
That Matter* (Houghton Mifflin, 2000)

Still Love in Strange Places: A Memoir (Norton, 2002)

*Seeing Past Z: Nurturing the Imagination
in a Fast-Forward World* (Norton, 2004)

GHOSTS
IN THE GARDEN

*Reflections on Endings, Beginnings,
and the Unearthing of Self*

BETH KEPHART

PHOTOGRAPHS BY WILLIAM SULIT

New World Library
Novato, California

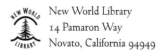
New World Library
14 Pamaron Way
Novato, California 94949

Front cover and text design by Mary Ann Casler
Typography by Tona Pearce Myers

Library of Congress Cataloging-in-Publication Data
Kephart, Beth.
Ghosts in the garden : reflections on endings, beginnings, and the unearthing of self /
Beth Kephart ; photographs by William Sulit.—1st ed.
    p.   cm.
Includes bibliographical references.
ISBN 1-57731-498-0 (hardcover : alk. paper)
1. Chanticleer Gardens (Wayne, Pa.)—Anecdotes. 2. Kephart, Beth. 3. Conduct of
life—Anecdotes. I. Title.
 SB455.K449 2005
 712'.5'0974814—dc22   2004023297

First printing, March 2005
ISBN 1-57731-498-0
Printed in Canada on partially recycled, acid-free paper
Distributed to the trade by Publishers Group West

10 9 8 7 6 5 4 3 2 1

For those who love the smell of the earth
and the color of a bloom upon a tree.

Hospitality is the fundamental virtue of the soil. It makes room.
It shares. It neutralizes poisons. And so it heals.
This is what the soil teaches:
If you want to be remembered, give yourself away.

— William Bryant Logan,
Dirt: The Ecstatic Skin of the Earth

Contents

Preface

*T*his book was written in a place called Chanticleer, among thirty-some acres of hills and native streams, tall trees, false ruins, shatteringly gentle peonies, and the architecture of lotus flowers trussed by opaque water. Chanticleer is a pleasure garden, so beautiful that it suggests the alchemy of danger, and the flowers there are tangled up inside each other, except where they've been disciplined to rows.

The first day I went to Chanticleer I would have said, about myself, that I was not yet old. The *old* hanging there like a gentle challenge. The *not yet* proof of a small talent for melodrama. It was April, my birthday; I was forty-one. I was a mother, a wife, a daughter, a sister, a friend, and I had come to the garden alone.

There was the immediate appeal of strangeness. The oddity of being lost a few miles from home. The air was cleaner, too, and the trees were pink eruptions, and it was pleasing to me, in ways I couldn't account for, that I did not know the names of most everything around me. This was tall and terminated in yellow. This was smug and hoarding its own fruit. This hadn't lifted its head toward the sun, but it was destined for a habit of pale purple. My lack of knowledge about the names of plants and trees was oddly clarifying. I wasn't responsible for adjudicating a thing. I was just there, on my birthday. Forty-one.

Later I would dream of going to the garden at night and sitting with it under the moon. Of waiting for owls, if there were owls, or for the bravura of any sleepless bird. White would be blue, I would imagine. Red would have long since succumbed. The water above the rocks would run toward amber wherever there was the memory of stars. Touch would be a tool, not a privilege. The mind would not cleave to what the eye could not see, and the heart would follow the pulse of a wing.

That would be later, much later. That would be after I had made it my habit to visit the garden every week. To drive the ten minutes from my house and park the car and follow the narrow ribbon of macadam down around and through the blooming things. I was drawn to the changeability of things. To how the clenched fist of a bud would grow suddenly generous and unfurl. To how something limp or pale would take a stand and intensify. I was drawn to the birds that were drawn to those trees and sang songs they never sang in my backyard. I was drawn to the murmur of the people passing by, to the shameless, even vulnerable way they spoke of their own wonder.

But perhaps I was drawn most deeply to the calm that I felt in the garden. I worried less when I was there. I felt less chased by deadlines and dilemmas. I grew more concerned with gains and gratitude than with losses. In the garden my age felt like a blessing. In the garden questions that had haunted me for years found quiet resolution. I learned the many parables of seeds and finally came to understand what the Czech writer Karel Čapek meant when he wrote these words of winter:

> Sometimes we seem to smell of decay, encumbered by the faded remains of the past; but if only we could see how many fat and white shoots are pushing forward in the old tilled soil...; how many seeds germinate in secret; how many old plants draw themselves together and concentrate into a living bud, which one day will burst into flowering life — if we could only see that secret swarming of the future within us, we should say that our melancholy and distrust is silly and absurd, and that the best thing of all is to be a living man — that is, a man who grows.

You can walk the loop of Chanticleer in twenty minutes, or you can choose a bench or a blanket of grass and sit there and wait for a bird, a thought, a cloud. At Chanticleer I did as I pleased — walking sometimes, at times almost running, often sitting on a hill of green or beneath a tree or right beside a stream. Looking, seeing, breathing, living. Being a woman who grows. I wanted, at times, to be planted in that ground. I wanted the face of a flower.

This is a book about land and about how land, like us, changes over time. It is a book about legacies and ghosts, a book about what happens when we recognize and honor the selves that, in the hurry of our lives, we've left behind. It is a book about our need to preserve the things we love, and our need to let them go. Lock a seed in a jar, and it will never grow. Nudge the seed into the soil, and if you wait and water and watch and have faith, there will be a bud.

The paradox that all writers come to is the paradox of details. Too few of them, and no story can feel true. Too many, and the story drowns inside its own conceit and expects too much from those who hear it. We want to tell stories that reverberate. We want to make our story plural. We want, as the great poet Pablo Neruda once wrote, "poetry worn away as if by acid by the labor of hands, impregnated with sweat and smoke, smelling of lilies and of urine, splashed by the variety of what we do, legally or illegally." We want to write as right as that. As meaningfully and as on purpose.

In choosing to write a book in a garden called Chanticleer, I am choosing, in some ways, to write about a particular place and time — about two years in a garden in that part of southeastern Pennsylvania that has been known, for a century now, as the Main Line. I am telling you about a spot of land that was once home to the Lenni-Lenape Indians, once surveyed by William Penn, once a working farm complete with barns and cows and horses, and, finally, beginning in the early years of the twentieth century, a beautiful but never arrogant estate. The gift of Chanticleer is the gift of one Adolph Rosengarten Junior whose father, a successful industrialist, had built the estate in 1913. Adolph Rosengarten grew up on the Chanticleer hills — picked apples from its trees, sledded down its hills, wandered freely in its streams. Briefly he went away to school, but when he returned he married a companionable woman named Janet and settled in a home that his father built for him there, on that estate. Adolph's love for that land was both pragmatic and poetic — he loved the trees, he loved the pond, he loved the vistas, he loved the quiet — and as he grew older, and as suburbia encroached, he vowed that nothing would destroy it. Chanticleer exists today because Adolph could not bear the thought of bulldozers flattening his childhood hills on behalf of cookie-cutter houses, could not tolerate the possibility of the land he loved being divided, clawed into, and subsumed. The gardens of Chanticleer exist today because a man who cared about legacy and life willed them into being, and yes, I have written about that particular place, during two particular years in my life.

But gardens are never frozen in time. They grow and spill and burst and fade, then cycle through again. Many gardeners now have put their hands into the soil of Chanticleer — turning a former tennis court into so many herbaceous borders, crowding the margins of a pond with fragrant colors, converting a cut-flower garden into a considered promenade, sneaking foreign things inside deeply luscious woods, letting watercress loose upon the surface of a stream. Many gardeners have put their hands into the soil of Chanticleer, and countless women and men and children have walked the thin macadam.

What happened to me at Chanticleer can happen to anyone anywhere — to anyone who takes a detour from routine and stops, at last, to search for answers to old questions: What will I do with the next portion of my life? What will I count among my blessings?

GHOSTS
IN THE GARDEN

The Sound of
Something Blooming

We come to gardens bearing memories of gardens. I came to Chanticleer remembering a fringe of strawberries that pressed up against my childhood home. Whether we ever actually ate the strawberries that those tousled plants bore, I don't remember. Whether my mother planted them there, or perhaps my father, I cannot say for sure. But I know I crouched the little girl's crouch and peered, the way children peer, toward the fruit. I know I loved how the red would follow white, and how the white had come from green, and how the pendant of juice, with its thistle of seeds, would plump until it was too fat for its serrated cap. There is nothing exotic about a strawberry patch except that it delivers on its promise.

A strawberry fringe is a garden to a girl, just as the creek that runs between the old shade trees across the street is a child's haven. I was the one who didn't mind mud in her shoes, the child who named the tadpoles, then the frogs. I was an ad-venturess at the creek across the street, where it was cool and dark and also many shades of green (moss, algae, leaves). In a year I would move with my family to an isolated outpost in Al-berta, Canada, where nothing anywhere was the lucky color of the Irish and I couldn't find a seed, and I grew determined — always, forever — never to see that much comatose brown again. Three months later we would be back home, in the house with the strawberry fringe. My toes in the creek. My hands on the frogs. My dreams of fruit and flowers.

I didn't know the names of stars; that was my brother's province. But I knew where to find the honeysuckle, and I knew the value of that single four-leafed clover. I knew something about the smell of tulips in the spring, and the sound of crick-ets was, for me, the sound of something blooming. It was just a feeling I had. It was just the memory that I neatly fashioned and hoarded for myself so that I'd have it to return to later, when I needed to remember the child I had been. She looked for turtles in her yard. She cuffed her trousers, tossed her shoes, got muddy feet. She collected mica, granite, snail shells, crystals, and she loved the daring dangle of a miniature strawberry. She was not concerned with what she did, only with what she found. She lived sun to sun and moon by moon, with unimpeded dreams.

Held in Suspense

*T*hat first day of April, when I went to Chanticleer, the promise of the garden was held mostly in suspense. There were the unburst buds of old magnolia trees and the tentative arrival of jack-in-the-pulpits in the woods. The daffodils had raised their shoulders on the hills, the cherry trees were almost pink, and there was a tincture of crocus purple in the grass. But mostly the message was: Wait and see; watch me. Like a memory just vaguely coming into view or the mist of a dream upon awakening, the garden in early April was all suggestion and seduction.

The beauty of a garden will be revealed in time. I walked the macadam path. Stood on the bridge. Crouched near the stream. Listened to the murmuring around me: wings, women, water. What next? I asked myself. What next? I was forty-one. My son was no longer a little boy, but an adolescent with his

own thoughts and agenda. I had been with my husband for nearly twenty years; how we loved and what we loved seemed entirely familiar. The work I strive to do didn't give me plea-sure anymore, and I was going nowhere, in a muddle in my mind. Can you find your purpose on a declivitous hill? Can you see beyond that turn, toward what's next? At points in the gar-den the path diverged. Go this way. Go that way. It was up to me to choose.

Dreaming Back the Past

Sometimes it's the going back that takes us forward. At Chanticleer I found myself leaning toward those memories that I had long ago set aside for me. I, the girl of the strawberry fringe, had been good (I walked and looked and remembered) at many enviable things. I had been good at floating on a raft at the edge of the sea. I had been good at skating on ponds — over twigs, beneath shadows, around frozen shoots of grass. I had been good at classifying the rocks I found as more or less hard, more or less smooth. I had been good at huddling with my brother during a sudden rush of rain, watching for the zig of yellow lightning. I had been good at sitting with my back against the bark of an old oak tree and writing poetry that no one would ever see. I had been good at these many things, and the sun, the air, the buds, the stream brought goodness back to me.

But it wasn't just my history that I found myself keeping company with in the garden. It was also (daringly, agreeably) the haunt of bobcats and black bear, the echoes of Lenni-Lenapes and Quakers, the evanescent fragments of vanished farmers and families. Standing alone at the top of one hill, I could almost hear the click of whelk in a wampum belt and the mating calls of ruffled goose. I could conjure the holler of a boy sledding the slopes and the sound of a gentleman's shoes on the walk and the sound of a blade striking stone beneath turf. I could tell myself tales about the first dark-eyed woman who spent a night beside the stream or found a bush of berries behind the trees beyond the hill. The gardener's obsession begins with the seasons. My thoughts, as I walked, were of ghosts.

Years and years and years ago — hundreds of years — breathing, living, longing, kneeling, praying, loving, sleeping, dreaming already took place on the land that would become Chanticleer. There were hands peeling the bark from trees and inscribing that bark with signs. There was the discovery of nuts, the skinning of deer for moccasins, the roasting of game over fire, the planting of maize, the settling in, and also pottery and arrowheads; dogs that did not bark but howled; blankets made of turkey feathers; and the fanciful use of porcupine quills. Wildcat, groundhog, and hare were not to be eaten. Corn could be prepared twelve different ways. Men and women were (imagine this) equal, and children waited six years to get a name. Years and years and years ago there were those who believed that when people passed away they took one soul with them on their journey to Sky World and left the other soul behind. What was this second soul for? To keep what once existed alive somehow. To appear, now and again, to a woman sifting histories in a garden.

I couldn't pin any of it down, of course. I couldn't say it happened just like that, right here. I couldn't say anything was for certain — not that day, and not for months. But later I discovered this: A gardener digging at Chanticleer once found — beneath leaf mold, between roots — an arrowhead. He cleaned it of its mud and slugs and took it home, for history's sake.

The past is kept where the past has been until it is dreamed back again.

Shortening the Distance

When you do not know the names of things, you fashion metaphors — a human instinct, as it turns out, and not strictly a poetic one. After my first trip to Chanticleer, I returned a week later, and a week after that until, weather permitting, it was my custom. I followed the macadam where the macadam led, measuring distances with my feet, trolling for metaphors. I came, without notable originality, upon music. Not looping refrain, not cheeping melody, but something I registered as symphony — woodwind, string, percussion, brass. Symphony being a generalization, of course, for jazz riffs in the garden too, and ribald discordancies, and there are parts of Chanticleer that strike a single, mournful note, just as there are stretches of green silence. But in the beginning, when I didn't have the words for things, *symphony* suited, it helped me explain the garden to myself. It helped me see between the stalks and leaves and slowly gain my footing.

I found overture in the tennis court, which is the garden's first event inside the gate. I found it in the play of flowers pulled through the court's stair rails, in the competing heights of the herbaceous borders, in the clang of colors of the dug-out central plots. At the farthest edge is a pergola, heavy with the ramble of roses, and this houses a bench as well as shade and provokes, among countless women younger than I, the inevitable *Imagine a wedding*. There is romance in the tennis court, the sound of the song of the future.

If you leave the tennis court and follow the path down and to the right, you enter the realm of violins. In the spring, eighty thousand pale narcissi to one side; in late summer, the lengthened tips of grasses to the other. It is neither the flowers nor the grasses that suggest the violin, but the way both defer to the wind; they defer completely. The slightest disturbance in the air, and everything bends then straightens then bends again: so many bows against the strings.

After that, to the right, are the strut and tempo of the cut-flower and vegetable garden. The flowers in rows. The vegetables in an enclosure. The upraised arms of espaliers — apples, pears — because something has to conduct this orchestra. There is the snap-snap of the kitchen here, the notion of *yield* that is ultimately inseparable from any domestic garden, the prudent percussion of anticipation.

The sonata is the garden by the serpentine stream, where ferns uncoil early and camas blues the mood. I hear oboe here, a solo performance. I hear the notes my brother played in the first house that I remember. He was thirteen or fourteen. I was eleven or twelve and of the mind that he could do anything. You can run and jump across this stream. You can walk a bridge across it. You can go back and forth, from bank to bank, and still the oboe's playing.

At the pond, it's the entire orchestra at once — goldfinches and hummingbirds, floating flowers and frogs, the bang and burst of color at the water's sculpted edge, and no protection from the sun. I have never analyzed it or fabricated an explanation. I have never separated the notes, or deconstructed the chords, or tried to figure out how one thing plays against the other. The pond roars, chimes, clamors, yearns. It is a hopeful sound that it seems to make, and also a caprice.

In the Asian Woods there is a pause, an interregnum, a silence; you take the shade, you catch your breath, you listen for the birds. Up the hill there is bel canto: sorghum and silver trees set down in a composition of fine curves. Farther up the hill (think of crescendo) is the old apple house, and after that (and here you have to lean forward and really climb before you reach it) there is the coda of the terrace, everything four cornered and squared, save for the flowers that grow up between the sidewalk cracks or spill from the profusion of old pots.

You trade what you can see for what it makes you hear, and somehow, on some days, you know a landscape slightly better. You imagine yourself into a place, and you are more fully there. Metaphor is only ever symbol. But metaphor, in its way, is the precursor of possession, a sideways step that shortens the distance between the unknown and the familiar.

A Talent for Living

*W*henever I went to the garden I was leaving work behind. Words and books, the writing life, the expectations others had of me. I was forsaking deadlines and logic, a liberation I had not realized, until that spring, that I was seeking. I was giving up on the notion that words alone can solve riddles. You can write yourself into your life, or you can write yourself directly out of it; I had been losing track of me. I had found myself measuring myself by my words, found myself too awfully focused on the need to get things right.

But you are never perfectly right when it comes to words. You are only yourself, and when you are alone as much as I had been alone with the work, yourself becomes too tight and stingy. You try to put too fine a point on things; you lose your talent for idle thought or lazy dreaming. You start doing battle with yourself over finally meaningless things when you could

and actually should be out helping your neighbor rake her leaves. You obsess (but of course you obsess) until the joy is gone from that thing you'd loved, until your fury overwhelms your passion, until you no longer know how to sit with your back against a tree and write poetry that no one will ever see. I had become a writer because I'd loved the sound, the kiss of words. But now language seemed vacuous and puny.

What I had loved had become what I felt compelled to do; it was time to walk out my own front door. "Keenly observed," author Gretel Ehrlich has written, "the world is transformed." I went to the garden to see more truly. I went for transformation's sake, and to win back my talent for plain living.

How Do You See Everything?

*O*ne day I went to the garden, and a stranger spoke to me. She was a small lady with a hunch in her back, and without needing to ask or know my name, she stood before me on the narrow path and started speaking: "I am afraid," she confided, looking up at me because she was so small, "that if I stay on the path I'll miss the stuff only the young ones get to see." She stopped there, paused, then continued. "But what if I go off the path," she said, "and can't remember where I left it? This is a problem too, I'm afraid. How do you see everything?"

She had a cane and thick sunglasses. She was alone and wore a crocheted jacket on a too-warm-for-jackets day. She was not asking idle questions because she didn't have the time to idle, and there I was, alone as well, on my own imperfect mission. Maybe I should have feigned confidence and promised that the carved-out path yields all. Or should have said: Off the path, in that direction, is a tree so big you could housekeep beneath it, and: Do what you must to cross the stream, and: There is a spot in the Asian Woods that is almost surely virgin, but don't think that's everything. I could have taken her elbow in my hand and led her to my own found places, but this lady wanted neither lies nor courtesies. She wanted an answer to her question, and she asked it again: "How do you see everything?" The challenge stood between us. She put her weight against her cane and, dignified, she waited.

I will be her, I thought to myself, in forty years. I will be her, with that slight hunch from a lifetime of bad posture, leaning on a cane instead of somebody's arm. We were independent women, at least we wanted to think we were, wanted to think we could go to a garden and be there by ourselves. It's not so hard — is it? — to get away. It's not so terribly incriminating. But to see *everything*. To know how to leave the path and where and when to get back on. To dare to lose ourselves, if only for a morning, in a garden, near a stream?

I felt the stranger's eyes on me, an impertinent stare through the shades, and suddenly I felt self-conscious about what I imagined she saw: a face grown prematurely hollow, pleats in the skin, eyes that must have been green just then, for I was standing in the sun. There's a certain threshold faces cross, a certain point in time when the face no longer summons history but instead forecasts the future; I passed that threshold a few years back. It's not something you forget, the first time you see your own face old. It's not something you can speak about until time heals the wound.

And yet, I thought, as I stood there with that lady: If I were younger, if there were less living in my eyes, less time, would this winter lady with the summer jacket have given me her question? Would she have thought me wise enough to understand her meaning, to balance it in silence before I proposed an answer?

"You know," I said at last, "there is no seeing everything."

"That's so," she sighed. "I know."

"I mean," I said, "you can get up close and study that one petal, but then you miss the flower. And you can stand on the hill and get the panoramic view, but then —"

"But then," she interrupted, "you miss the bees." Her eyes were still lost to me behind the shades. Her weight put too much pressure on the cane.

"Something like that," I said.

"Yes," she said. "Something indeed." Moments passed. She was still standing there, looking about her, testing the limits.

"How much time do you have?" I asked her, at last.

"The morning, if I'm lucky," she said.

"Leave the path," I told her. "Leave it. Absolutely."

The Drowning Girl

I didn't find the girl until I myself left the path and crossed the finger of the stream and stood where I could really see. It was June, I think, and the water in this secondary pond was clear, and there was no one else around but me and this girl in the pond, this cast-stone girl. Someone had submerged her so that only the top of her head was dry. The rest of her — her eyes, her mouth, her breasts, her hands, her elegant legs, her delicate toes, the waist of her skirt, its hem — was sunk below the water line.

I sat down on the grass at the edge of this pond, pulled blades of green between my fingers, and gave myself over to studying her: how she could be so alive and yet submerged. How she could be that alone but for the minnows. All my life I have been moved by antique photographs, and she was like that in my eyes, so sepia and white and still. She was like that, but there was more. The pond was small and round, after all. And water reflects, just like glass.

What does it mean to nest a girl so deep inside a pond? To put her there and leave her, so that she might be found again? She reaches, this cast-stone being, with long slender arms. She gathers the minnows to her, but they are independent creatures. She sits and she waits and there is green within her hair — a slick patina — for this is what age looks like, in a pond.

After I found the girl, I went often to see her, sometimes leaning so far over the pond that my face was floating there beside hers. I took a strange comfort from her eternal peacefulness, the way she simply let the minnows go and refused to fuss about the green in her hair. Escaping words and work, as I was, escaping the knots I had tied my life into, escaping the overwhelming sense that my future was uncertain, I found the girl's easy way with her own circumstance intoxicating. All I had to do was go and let her graces find me.

Keeping the Land Alive

I was thirteen when my parents sold the house with the strawberry patch and moved to that part of Pennsylvania where the Lenni-Lenapes had once settled themselves — pulling fish from the streams in baskets they wove, sitting down with their Three Sisters (squash, corn, and beans), conjuring supernatural powers to keep bad things from smoking up their souls. The year was 1973, and my family's new house was custom-built on a bend in the road; from my bedroom I saw trees. I don't think any of us was attuned to residual spirits or thought to dig for arrowheads. I didn't go looking for a new brown creek; I didn't set out a box of food for turtles. I thought about the new house, the new neighborhood, the bus route, and friends; I was immune to the history of the land.

But all this time, Adolph Junior was right down the road, not even ten minutes away. He was where he was and where

he'd steadfastly been since he was a boy, alert to the sound of the saw. Thin and already in his sixties, he was hard at work at Chanticleer, consolidating acreage, putting trust into a will, doing all he could to preserve a swath of land in a suburbaniz-ing county. He would keep the spirit of the land alive. He would set earth aside and in that way make room for memory.

I drove for years on the roads that fork at Chanticleer, but I never looked beyond the fence, I never wondered. I went away for a spell, then returned. Moved back to where I'd come from — ten minutes, again, from Chanticleer, though ten min-utes on different roads. Much had changed since I'd been gone. Farms I thought I could count on had vanished, the spaces be-tween houses had been halved, and halved twice more. And I was different too, I was busy — consumed with being a mother to my son, consumed with words and work when he was gone.

By then it was 1994, and Adolph Junior had passed away. In his absence, a British horticulturist was bringing color to the land, wrenching the poison ivy out at the roots, converting tennis courts into sunken gardens, planting thousands of bulbs like a river down one hill. He was hollowing gourds and setting them out for the birds. He was thinking about sight lines be-tween trees. He was thinking about the paint box of flowers, the music of flowers, the theatrics of flowers, and about swales, sculpture, and mood. He would come to hate the word *whimsy*, preferring *edgy* or *alive*. He would come to think that the pond that merely reflected trees and sky needed a crowd of blooms along each side. He would root in a bush, then tame it back. He would stake things up until they were strong enough to stand on their own.

And this is how the garden grew, but I knew nothing of it. Drove by almost every day and did not turn my head, did not hear the bulbs cracking open in the spring or the ferns pushing up through the dark. I didn't give a second's thought to gardeners in boots and gloves or tools and trucks, or to the possibility of seeds, or to the girl I'd once been. I was crowded into the space of my life, writing and mothering and mothering and writing and holding on hard to the depleting idea that time is an enemy and that *things had to get done*. I had not yet found the earth again, or maybe I was buried. But there was never an afternoon alone set aside for creeks. There was never an idle search for a clump of ripe strawberries.

The Season We Were In

I took my son to the garden that first season. We were hardly through the gate before he took off down the path and flew. "See you, Mom," he said, and he was running, as if the garden were a racetrack and some crowd was circled round and roaring. He had big feet already, and I could hear them pounding, pounding, pounding, turning the corner, disappearing. He must have thought Chanticleer was so much larger than it is. He must have thought he needed speed and wings to see it.

I trailed behind him at a mother's pace. Some of the flowers still kept secrets, hiding their buds behind leaves, not letting on. The hydrangeas were in full force, though, and the bromeliads were happy among the other tropicals, and the trees were abundantly green and sweet, standing there like

umbrellas to shield us from the sun. Everyone I passed was looking up at the trees or reaching out to touch the most vulnerable parts of them. I don't remember there being much talk, but I do remember mothers with daughters, and daughters with mothers, of almost every age.

Up ahead of me and then behind me, my son ran — the sound of his shoes announcing his arrival. "Hey, Mom," he said, and then he was by me again, sprinting past, while I was only just turning the corner of the pond and heading across the bridge toward the Asian Woods, where everything was green and dark, almost (you could kid yourself) primordial. Through the woods and up the hill, toward the original estate — the first house, Adolph Senior's house, with its formal, terraced garden and its roofed-over but open-to-the-breezes porch. You could tell it was going to be a big season for hydrangea and that the peonies would soon have plenty to say. You could tell a lot, or you could anticipate; such was the season we were in.

My son was threatening to run another lap around me, but this time he stopped and walked beside me. Just slowed down, so that now in the garden there was this mother and her son, not talking much, just looking up, mostly at the trees. He was breathing hard, and I was not. He was my height, since I wore shoes with tall heels. And if neither of us knew the names of things, we weren't pretending to. I was twenty-nine when he was born, and this was twelve years later. My face had changed, and my body had too, and I already understood that we were ghosts just passing through. But I didn't let on. I would not say, *Right now will be a memory soon.*

Later, during subsequent visits, he would go off the path, cross over the stream, find me again, then disappear. He would set off like some kind of spy on some kind of mission, then return with the news of his adventures. There was a woodshed in the Asian Woods. Had I seen it? No. There was an alley between the grasses that was full of bumps; he'd found it. There was a leopard-patterned chair, where he had stopped to sit, and why were his feet wet? Because he'd walked across the stream. Across it? Through it. It's not that deep. It's shallow.

He saw the jerseys of his favorite soccer team in the bed of orange flowers; this is what he said. He saw the lists of plants that the gardeners left in boxes as clues to an urgent mystery. It was all a game to him, his own private game, though we had come together and we would leave together — not often, but sometimes.

He was tall, slim, dear, this son of mine. I walked behind him, listened to him, looked for him in the shaded places. He was turning the garden into his own narrative, even as I had begun to work it into mine.

Remember This?

One day I took my mother to the garden. It was a warmish day; just us. She made her way slowly down the gentlest decline (holding my arm, sometimes touching tree branches), then chose a bench beneath a tree inside the woods. I sat beside her, and between us fell a triangle of sun. A gardener was at work across the path; people walked by. We sat there peacefully, my mother and I, a wedge of yellow sun between us, but otherwise in shadow. We talked of nothing much, and it was good. We said, every once in a while, Remember this? Remember that? We talked about how the branches of one tree reached toward another and formed an arch. We talked about how high vines will climb if they're rooted in good soil.

Things were blooming in the Asian Woods.

There was so much color in the shadows.

Present Tense

*T*he more I went to Chanticleer,
the more I thought about what John McPhee has written
about earthly inconstancy:

At a given place — a given latitude and longitude —
the appearance of the world will have changed too
often to be recorded in a single picture, will have been,
say, at one time below fresh water, at another under
brine, will have been mountainous country, a quiet
plain, equatorial desert, an arctic coast, a coal swamp,
and a river delta, all in one Zip Code. These scenes
are discernible in, among other things, the sedimen-
tary characteristics of rock, in its chemical composition, magnetic components, interior color, hardness,

fossils, and igneous, metamorphic, or depositional age. But as parts of the historic narrative these items of evidence are just phrases and clauses, wildly disjunct. They are like odd pieces from innumerable jigsaw puzzles.

The land that I had come to trust didn't always pitch, then flatten, didn't always catch the rain in mild fissures, didn't always have a moon nearby — quartered, halved, or whole. Once it was home to a school of some extinct something — it must have been — and isn't there a better-than-average possibility that it was brushed by a fallen chunk of star? Earth is not constant. The garden will yield: Something will crumble, or something will fold. A herd of antelope will swoop in, or birds will drop exotic seeds, or the stream will break free of its walls, and the garden will become something new again, transformed.

Everything is held in the moment at Chanticleer. Everything is present tense, an outrageous act of courage. No two days at the garden will ever be the same; no two moments will, none of it can be perfectly preserved, and this, I think, makes Adolph Rosengarten's will an even more audacious proposition. He left what he loved not in a vault somewhere, not in a museum behind glass, not in a book sealed safe with covers, but out in the weather, in the rain and the sun, out in the open, subject to seasons and the fancies of new gardeners, to the interpretations and assumptions of those coming to terms with life's big questions.

Optimism

*G*retel Ehrlich believes that "lovers, farmers, and artists have one thing in common, at least — a fear of 'dry spells,' dormant periods in which we do no blooming, internal droughts only the waters of imagination and psychic release can civilize. All such matters are delicate of course. But a good irrigator knows this: too little water brings on the weeds while too much degrades the soil the way too much easy money can trivialize a person's initiative."

It was the end of July, hot weather. It hadn't rained for many days. Now when I went to the garden I'd sit at the bottom of the hill with a book on my lap — sometimes reading, sometimes just looking out on things: a gathering of bees, the sleepy drooping of big leaves, the geometry of the pebble garden that cascaded away from the so-called ruins, down toward the pond.

The gardeners, I came to see, were indefatigable. No matter how hot the sun shone or how little rain had fallen, they were there in their gray-green T-shirts and bandannas or broad-rimmed hats — snipping things, breaking into things, lifting things, transplanting. They moved here and there with their carts and their wheelbarrows, went one way, toward the shed, then returned with new hand tools. Stepping back, they took measure, then knelt down close again. The gardeners were ruthless when it came to weeds and undaunted otherwise.

What was so methodical about the gardeners was also what was peaceful: They did what they did as if time were on their side; they took some kind of solace from the heat of that long season. There's water beneath the surface of the earth, a medicinal wetness that works its way between stones and into fissures. At the height of heat that summer, the gardeners trusted the water they couldn't see. They took the pulse of the soil that they worked, moistened where they had to, gathered their tools, walked down the hill, then looked back up, and through it all, they kept their faith in blooming.

I sat where I sat, in a leopard-spotted chair, beneath the shade of a big old tree that must have been standing there for years (through summer's heat, through winter's ice, through a succession, now, of gardeners). When the gardeners disappeared for lunch, I went to see what they'd been doing. I crouched down low, as they had crouched, and touched their optimism.

Green for Us

Says architect Louis Kahn, "In every thing that nature makes, nature records how it was made. In the rock is a record of how the rock was made. In man is the record of how man was made."

One day I went to the garden and found a man alone up on one hill, looking out on things. Time had written itself deeply into his face; his eyes were not as bright as I imagine they had been. "I'm looking at the beauty," he told me, as I walked by, and so I stopped to stand with him. The narcissi had long since been deadheaded. The trees were a chlorophyll green. "Beautiful, isn't it?" he said, and I said, "Yes. It certainly is."

Then we stood silently some more until he told me a little of his life. He was the father of nine, he said. He had been married for many years. He'd been driving buses since he couldn't remember when, but what he loved was nature. "I love the beauty of things," he said. "I love the birds and clean air."

And so this man who had spent his lifetime driving buses had saved up what he could. Kept saving and saving until he had stowed away enough to buy a wedge of the Appalachians. "You ever been there?" he said, and before I could answer he went on, "It's all nature there. And birds. And air. It's the land I always wanted."

"That's nice," I said.

"Yes," he said. "A nice idea. But then my wife got sick, too sick to travel, and I'm up here, and the land's down there, and we see nothing of each other."

"I'm sorry," I said.

"Bad luck," he said. "I should have bought it earlier. Taken a risk. You have to live when you can."

He stopped speaking then. Just looked down the hill and exhaled. I looked at him while he looked at the garden, watched while this afternoon at a garden wrote its record into him. "It's real nice," he said. "Isn't it?"

"It is."

"They keep it so clean here. And green."

"They keep it that way for us," I said.

"Is that so?" he said.

"It is."

When We Were Young, Like Them

*O*ne day two kids went flying down the hill. Rumbling on their sides like tumbleweed. And then there were two more after them and yet another pair, and at least two mothers calling from behind. The story had been set in motion. The kids would not stop until the hill lost its slope; they would go tumbling as far as they could.

"Come back here," one mother called, but her words went unheeded.

"Don't go too far," another said. But the kids were laughing, tumbling, rumbling down, smearing their light pants with grassy green, taking the earth on their skin. Tufts of loosened stuff flew up. Things got twirled into their hair. Bugs with wings and bugs without scrambled as fast as they could.

"We're flying," the kids kept calling (though they were rolling on their sides).

"Don't go too far," their mother said.

But there was still plenty of slope for the kids, plenty of speed to be had.

I did that once, I thought, watching — a long time ago, on other hills, in other places, with my brother, with my sister, and alone. I did that once, and more than once, and so did my son.

I watched the kids roll and the mothers call. I saw one mother finally sprint down the hill and another stay right where she'd been, bemused, hands on her hips. At home, my own child was doing his own favorite things. Kicking the soccer ball around outside or writing stories at the kitchen table or reading some elaborate mystery. Flopping across the living room couch, tracing the patterns in the carpet. "I'm going to the garden," I had said before I left, and he'd said, "I'll see you, Mom."

"Do you want to come?" I'd asked him.

"Got things to do," he'd said.

"See you in an hour," I told him.

"Something like that," he'd said, and smiled.

I had closed the door behind me then, and we were both off, on our own. For this, too, is the thing about middle age: Motherhood shifts and changes. Suddenly other people's children don't just remind you of yourself. They remind you of the child you've loved, when he was young, like them.

Riding the Breeze

Seeds will ride the breeze. They will travel in the belly of a bird or float across the sea. Stay stowed away in a nest of leaves until a big wind blows, or be carried off then shaken loose from the pelt of a fox or hare. Friends send seeds and gardeners hunt them, and they are dust or they are huge, and they want the prick of a sharp knife, or they flinch from it. They will lie dormant all through winter, stay suspended in a paper sleeve, appear not to breathe in a sealed glass jar, but give seeds oxygen, moisture, the right temperature, light, and they won't be seeds anymore. They'll be what the genes have programmed them to be — roots wriggling out into the ground, other parts reaching for the sun, morphing into stigma and stamen, erupting, shamelessly, with petals.

Whether you are on the path or off it at Chanticleer, it's hard to accept the wholly unlikely fact that, for eons, nothing bloomed at all; there were no flowers. No public erotica, few paint-box colors, no anthers flecking off their grains of life.

The world had to wait for the dinosaur to exit stage left before it got the gift of flowers (so naturalist Loren Eiseley tells us), and flowers were self-serving from the start: Come take me, touch me, smell me, eat me, take my future with you. Self-serving but at the same time selfless too — the flower needs to give up its fruit to survive another season.

Blessings

*G*ardens are flowers tamed. They are seeds protected and hoped through, projected forward and disciplined. They are man and woman stepping in, and almost any metaphor applies: Gardens are music, gardens are a canvas, they are sacraments and sacrifice. Dominion is the oldest question in a garden. Beauty is the oldest idyll of man. A gardener has to decide, when she takes up her trowel, how much she will trust to the instincts of the seed, how much she will mess with the rules.

At Chanticleer, you could frame a thousand paintings, and that first summer I noticed how many people did, arriving with tubes of color, portable easels, and brushes in rubber bands. Most wore hats and sat on slightly tremulous stools, and they were keen, it seemed to me, on the mix of relatively fixed and forever transient things: the green waterwheel beside

the stream. The stone field house near the pond. The old storage shed that smells of apples and is carved out of the hill.

Keenly observed the world is transformed. Don't wait too long to see. The turquoise needle of an insect sits on a leaf that does not stir. A frog appears from the slick of one pond. A bluebird abandons a shelf upon the tree.

A flower blisters.

Another Way of Seeing

*P*lace can superimpose its intelligence over ours if we relinquish and give in. Place can shift perspective. The questions start to change. The values do. The hues. There is another way of seeing, always. You have to open to it.

Week after week I went to Chanticleer, mostly alone. I'd take an apple with me, eat it. I'd smooth out a seat on the grass and watch grass grow. I'd take a book and press open a page and then leave it to the sun. I'd sit in a swarm of butterflies until they'd forget I was there, and I would try to catch the scent of things and give them similes. This one smells like licorice. This one could be Kool-Aid. This one could be my mother's dress, hung up on the line to dry.

And some would say that I accomplished nothing, but I would say, looking back, that the opposite is true. I would say that I was learning to trust what I could not set in language, keep, control, or hold. I would say that I was learning to surrender. To stop warring with myself, to stop needing to be right, to come to terms with shifts and change, to sit on a hill and count my blessings.

And I would say as well that by the time September came and October edged toward November, I had come to understand that at Chanticleer they are not afraid to let things die. By the stream the once-tall ferns became a flattened molten brown, and that's all they were — exhausted and unashamed. In the pond the lilies lost their pink but glowed. In the vegetable garden the gourds grew overheavy for their vines and sagged. And elsewhere the cornstalks singed, while the reds yielded to yellows, while the leaves on the crabapple trees took off, leaving nothing but the berries. Fewer birds were in the trees, less song, and the bees began to cluster in odd places. Fewer people were passing through, and those who were there when I was spent less time looking for their faces in the mirror of the pond.

The gardeners, though — the gardeners worked their gardens. Tamped things down, harvested seeds, drew blankets over that which needed blankets. The gardeners went about doing what gardeners do. Respectful of the season.

"All changes, even the most longed for, have their melancholy," novelist Anatole France once wrote, "for what we leave behind us is a part of ourselves; we must die to one life before we can enter another."

Letting Go

I went to Chanticleer the very last day, before they closed the gates. I stood alone, under changeable skies, and thought about the seasons. About work and love and being a mother. About letting go and letting be. Take a breath, I told myself. Stand on this hill, and breathe.

Surviving Winter

*W*inter was white wind and ice. Whatever color survived, whatever seeds bulged underground, whatever plants kept the flame of their blooms in the greenhouse was, for voyeurs like me, completely out of view. Chanticleer was closed, and the nurturing of its gardeners went on beyond locked gates.

Still, on days when two sweaters and hot chocolate could do nothing against the chill, I dreamed of the garden in winter. I dreamed of the bulbs in the ground, biding their time. Of the birdhouse gourds knocking around in the wind. Of the espaliers still posing against the walls, naked, for the most part now, exposed with no way to run. I dreamed of Adolph Rosengarten, the boy, sledding down the steepest hill, and of Adolph the man, who gave the neighbors' children free run of the hill when it was no longer his time to fly. I thought of the ice pond and how it served the estate for years (How did they crack the ice? How did they transport it? How did it glisten?). I thought of Adolph's dog, Becka, a corgi, keeping her nose above the drifts while Adolph, an even older man now, walked the property, cane in hand, hat on his whitened head. He was, in my mind's eye, thinking ahead. He was still and continuously getting on in years. The past spooling through him like an old home movie. And the future? The future? Always in question.

Turn any dream into a globe and tilt it upside down, and there's your crystal snow. Put white-wax candles on windowsills, if you wish, and string lights across spruce trees, and seat forty people around the table on Christmas day. Put a man in a garden in conversation with himself, because if you have dreamed it, it somehow is. A garden is flowers tamed, seeds protected, music, sacrifice. A garden is a winter's dream, and it is also, always, fiction.

What Are Seeds For?

*D*uring the winter of my forty-first year, my friends sent seeds. Four-o'clocks and larkspur. Columbine and red flanders poppy. Love-in-a-mist. In jars, in sleeves, sometimes with instructions. *Keep dry. Keep cool. Think about the weight of dirt on each seed's head before you plant it in the spring.*

I never saw them coming. Didn't know what to do with so many seeds, especially in winter, especially since the garden I'd been caring for would never be my own. The four-o'clock seeds were round, brown, finite, hard in my hand, so self-contained. The columbine were shiny as spilled oil and less perfectly defined. The castor bean was ingeniously designed, its spotted skin like some smooth version of a calico cat's fur, and the sweet pea was similar in sheen to the dull lead of an old bullet I once saw in a Civil War display, only much smaller and much more perfect in its roundness.

But the jar of seeds that Susan sent was my museum of wonders, my very own vacuum-sealed curiosity shop of nettles and pods and Chinese lanterns, or things that looked like that. Whoever doubts the existence of God has not held this jar of seeds in her hands, has not held it up to the light and turned it and turned it and tried to find some means of explaining, some willfulness with words. You can evoke science, but that won't tell the story. You can say that a seed is nothing more than this: a plant embryo all tucked inside a handsome, tailored coat.

But to look at a seed and to appreciate the absolute suspense of it, to comprehend the *what if* nature of its quixotic enterprise, to *convey* it — well, you have to be both wise and bold, you have to avoid the grandiose, you have to step just shy of the cushy and sentimental. Seeds are hardly rare or strange. They are as commonplace as life. They can be gathered, as the seeds in Susan's jar were gathered, by a child named Rosette.

"What are the seeds for?" my son asked me one day.

And I said, "They are for planting."

And I meant, They are for hoping through. For believing in. For watching.

Individuated

I returned to the garden in my forty-second year, having dreamed of it in winter, having mapped it in my mind, having slipped a few friends' seeds into the earth near my front door, and having left a knot of projects on my desk. If I couldn't write well, I wouldn't write for now. If I was trying to sort things out, I would just wait until things got sorted. If I was thinking I could gauge what motherhood and passion should look like now, I would not draw any premature conclusions.

Now the way the land slid away and steadied was familiar to me. Now the song of the narcissi could be anticipated. And the way the stream snaked, and the way the Asian Woods gave shade, and the way the benches whiled away the time beneath the branches of big trees.

The revelations lay in the individuated things — in the phenomenon of inflorescence, in the frog that appeared between my feet, in the eager shoots of green beside the pond, and by the terrace, in the deep water bowl on the porch where they float fresh-cut flowers, never the expected flowers, always something stranger.

When you know one thing, you are free to learn another. When you breathe, you taste the air. I knew the sweep, the feel, the sound of Chanticleer. I wanted more than what I'd come to know. I wanted, now, to put a name to things, to fill my head with other people's stories.

The Sound of Spades

This is the way that Adolph
Rosengarten Junior walked the gentleman's estate that would
someday become a pleasure garden: nestling his hat on his
head (a touring hat, it has been said), taking up his cane in
his left hand (a strictly ornamental cane until a cane was nec-
essary later), and beckoning to Becka, who may or may not
have been on leash. Leaving through the porch of Minder
House, his home, and looking to the left, where his wife Janet's
flowers — sweet William, foxglove, tulips, begonias in the
spring and summer, field-grown mums in the fall — formed a
pastel edge in the nearby garden that he double-trenched himself. Heading down the slope toward the pond that was still, in
this era, rimmed with nothing but big trees. This would be
early morning, 7:15. This would be a man alert to weather and
the season, a man whose favorite word was *tilth* and who liked

to say, to those he trusted, that the fourth dimension of land-scape art is time. He was concerned, always, with time.

Down toward the pond, then. Down toward that place where the slope breaks away into a rather steep decline and where once stood the soft-stone farmhouse of the farmers who owned the property before the Rosengartens did. What he was appreciating then was the general sweep of things, the generous wide open-ness of the land, the tall trees beyond. What he was doing was seeing.

He'd swing around the front of his house after that, for he had stood in one place long enough. Go down to the end of the drive to collect the morning's *New York Times* and check on the dark green wheel beside the stream that powered the play-ful water features (there was a spilling teacup; there was a driz-zling vase; there was a fascination, always, with how water moved and rebuked constraints). Go farther, past the ice pond and toward the potting shed, where his gardeners would by now have gathered and be waiting for the news. *The Missus will need cut flowers for a dinner party at six. The Missus will want string beans for dinner. Idle hands make work for the devil. Rome wasn't built in a day.*

Leave the gardeners to their tools and their machines, to their pot-bellied stove, which would be fired up for the sake of heat, if heat, that is, were needed. Head farther up the hill, in the direction of his sister's house (which would be to his left) and his parents' house (to his right), or at least that's how he thought about these mostly empty buildings now. Straight up the drive between the two houses, to the very end of it, where Church Road divided his acreage from the acreage across the way, from the prize-winning herds of Ayrshire cattle, from the rolling hills and grand estate of Ardrossan Farms, from Hope Montgomery Scott herself, upon whose life *The Philadelphia Story* had been fashioned (she had danced with Winston Churchill on Onassis's yacht; she had seduced and loved and lived). Across Church Road were myth and splendor, and, more than that, bucolic land, and if anyone was near enough to hear Adolph say it, he would opine, while looking out on this, that he'd been born a lucky man.

The sound of spades in earth would be behind him now. The sound of shears on stems. The smell of three hundred and fifty rose bushes, if roses were in season. The thought in his head of this Sunday past, when he and Janet had picnicked on the lawn, taking the vegetables straight from their own garden, ten thousand foot square, choosing only the smallest, least starchy of vegetables for the diabetic Janet, lima beans the size of fingernails. Or he would be thinking of that passage he just had read or recently remembered, tugging on a line from *Vanity Fair* or *David Copperfield* or from that book — what was the

name of it? — about aesthetic gardening. He would be thinking that it was time to head back to the house, and to his wife
and to the work that waited on his desk.

Later he would take an apple from a barrel in the apple
house, peel away its wax paper, and eat it to the core, tossing
the seeds and the stem to a happy squirrel. Later he would
climb into his Plymouth (just a Plymouth, never a Mercedes)
and ask his driver to take him into town, or to the board meet-
ing at the hospital, or to the library, where he liked to read
French plays. He did not dress like wealth. He was opposed to
showiness. He liked you if he trusted you, and he trusted those
who stood for something.

This was the early 1970s. This was a few years after the
boyfriend of a maid put a bullet in a cavity just below his heart
while he was sitting in his office reading, just sitting there reading on a day that had begun like any other. This was when his
gardening staff was limited to three: the two old brothers who
had come up from West Virginia in the 1920s and found enduring employment with the Rosengartens and a third much
younger man who sported long hair and had stood on prin-
ciple against the Vietnam War. It was to the younger gardener
that Adolph began to speak about legacies and land. It was of
him that he asked the question, What will bring people to this
place when I am gone? There was an ecological garden down

the road. There were arboreta famous for their trees. There were huge gardens that spread over acres and acres and offered summer theater, orchid houses, woods in which one walked for miles.

But Chanticleer, and its thirty-odd acres? Chanticleer, and its indigenous plants? Would meadows and ornamental grasses make it enduring, lasting, special? Would espaliers of apple, pear, blue atlas cedar? And if they started right now, slowly letting the public in, slowly hosting horticulturists, slowly opening the gates, would they come to know how others viewed this land? About how it might be loved and why, when Adolph no longer walked across it?

They respected each other, this man with the money and this man with the long hair. They walked the property and walked the property and tried to see the future. And as the years went by and the elderly brothers retired and Adolph leaned more heavily into his cane, Adolph began to speak of something new, to wonder out loud about pleasure gardens. He bought a book about them and shared it with the young gardener. He walked around considering the power of the picturesque. He started coming home from his trips to Holland, France, and England with stories about gardens that weren't afraid to be exotic. And the young gardener who loved the grasses and the espaliers and the native blooming things of Chanticleer began to see and to understand that the future wasn't the future he'd been planting. The future was something different now, some-thing more daring and painterly, something less indigenous, perhaps even immodest. It was time to bring another gardener on board, another gardener or two, one of them British.

Consider the Gardeners

The two brothers who came from West Virginia banked the stream with stones. The young gardener who had objected to the war trained trees to keep their branches low. Adolph himself designed a silt trap and a filter system to keep the pond water clean, and long before any of this, when Adolph was still a boy, a landscape architect named Thomas Sears had designed the terrace that still sits upon the hill.

Gardens are the beneficiaries and victims of time, yet some things do remain. Some marks are more indelible than others, some gestures keep their muscle. The second year I went to the garden I was inclined to consider the gardeners, to watch them work, to accept the names they shared with me, to follow the line of their thinking. A gardener in the Asian Woods taught me something of plant division. A gardener on the terrace drew big leaves aside to point out small ones. A gardener stood on the top of the hill, looked both ways, and then started flying — down the hill he went, taking these big gorgeous unrestricted strides, as if such running were not child's play but the right of any gardener.

"What are you doing?" I would sometimes ask them, and the gardeners would stop and tell me — I am thinning this, I am trying this, I am looking for this, I am experimenting, I am caught off guard by the eyes of this hungry praying mantis, I am encouraging this vine, I am speculating about the stream, I am standing here, thinking. And if some other visitor came along with questions of her own, those questions too got answered, or considered, anyway. Will this tree grow in sun as well as shade? Is this flower a hybrid of this thing and the other? If I take these seeds and plant them in clingy clay, will they have the temerity, the tenacity, to push out roots and grow? Is this the same version of the tree that I think once grew at the edge of my grandfather's farm? And how is it that you get bluebirds here? I hardly see them anymore. And how is it that when I plant that thing I get nothing but leaves and roots?

What struck me then and strikes me now is the generosity of gardeners who daily work the soil. The way they give away what they know because they don't own it in the first place. No hoarding of secrets here, no claiming beauty as one's own, no miserly inclination to hide the bud that's burst to bloom. You can't see everything, you never do. But a gardener will broaden your perspective, if you allow a gardener to.

Surrender

They took down the house where Adolph Rosengarten Junior lived, and they replaced it with false ruins. Between the new stone walls they fit a long stone table, and on the floor and sills they scattered books of heavy stone. There is a pool in these ruins, and in that pool are stone faces that do not float but appear to float and are pink and white and gray and also brushed with algae. Water streams in — translucent sheets, like liquid paper — and then the water stops.

I know a little girl who believes that the ruins are inhabited by monsters. I have heard one person explain to another that the faces are alive or that they are dying, that they are asleep or that they are waking, that they are old or that they are young, or that they're just stone, they are just stone. I have heard women deploring the shape of the unforgiving mouths and making declarations against the blot of algae on the brows.

"Imagine those faces five years from now," one woman said to another, meaning, Do not imagine my own.

I don't suppose that Adolph himself foresaw the erasure of his house on behalf of roofless, glassless ruins. I don't think that when he looked ahead he imagined children naming the monsters in a pool, or women standing in his naked living room, or grown men arranging themselves in the ruins' thronelike chairs; I've seen one fall asleep there, as if a guest of Adolph's, perhaps a cousin. "Could be worse," the man confided, before he drifted off to dreaming, and I suppose it could. But I don't suppose that Adolph imagined that man sitting there when he left his land to others.

The apple trees Adolph loved are gone, the big pond at the base of the hill is now a ricochet of color, the flowerbeds Adolph dug himself have been replaced with other things, and, furthermore, you cannot turn the pages of stone books. Trees grow where Adolph's wife once stood — along with buckets of cacti, delicate moss. Children tell each other fairy tales, and grown men snore while their wives go off to sniff the blue hydrangea. *Legacy* is another word for *gift*. And also (I use the word again) *surrender*.

As Pure as That

An acorn made of polished stone is lodged in one of the books of stone at the ruins. Nothing more than an acorn (no sprawl of words, no pictures), as if stories were as pure as that, as gorgeous and straightforward. I would like to write a book (a page) that is an acorn only. That ripens from green to brown and supposes a tree, yielding something like a garden.

The Science of Division

When my son went with me to the garden during my forty-second year, it was to look for shade in heat, or to escape the bees that had started hiving in our house. Even when I wore my tall shoes we could no longer see eye to eye; that's how much he had grown in hardly any time. He looked down on me and laughed as he did. "I'm a man now, don't you think?" he'd say. And then go on his way.

Sometimes we'd rendezvous beneath the skirt of a tree that we had found the year before. An off-the-path tree that offered an apron of shade and into which someone — a gardener, it had to be — had inserted two comfortable chairs. We were reading that summer — *Of Mice and Men*, *To Kill a Mocking-bird* — reading when we sat there, thinking out loud, turning the pages. The talk kept coming back to justice, to what is right and wrong, to the responsibility of fathers and friends, to prejudice and fate. My son was of his own mind on all this. I didn't debate him. I didn't instruct him. I said what I thought to be true, and he gave his version, and no one was right and no one was wrong; there was no burden of persuasion, no complicated deadline. Simple talk, in a garden, beneath a tree, while the sun burned hot beyond us.

Give seeds oxygen, moisture, the right temperature, light, and they won't be seeds anymore. They'll be the child before you who thinks he's a man, who stands taller than you do, who contests your idea of justice, who has his own things to pay attention to, his own obsessions, his own array of moods, his own changeable reactions to the sun, the heat, the shade, his own notions about words and books and acorns. If the idea of this had somehow made me feel unsteady on my feet before — if I had anticipated, tallied, and imagined losses; if I had tried to write my way in and out of it — I wasn't mourning over losses anymore. I was learning the science of division from the gardeners of Chanticleer; I was learning the art of breathing. I was learning that loving the full beauty and force of a bloom means having the good sense not to quash it.

White as Blue

*O*ne day I went to the garden and there was a breeze, and the clouds were sailboating the sky. The tall grasses were copper colored at the base and tufted with white-purple. The evergreens were a darker green, standing, as they were, beneath a slightly different sky. I stood on the hill above the pond, watching hummingbirds scout out nectar. The flowers on slender stalks leaned left. The dragonflies revved their motors.

There were big white butterflies, like airborne handkerchiefs.

There were men in good shoes, with their hands behind their backs.

There was a game of hide-and-seek and mothers talking with mothers.

There were lovers hand in hand on the paths, some of them young, some not young at all.

The painters were doing what painters do when they come to a garden hunting for vision. The walkers were taking their walks. The gardeners for their part were busy (earth on their knees, earth in their hands), and I was alone, remembering the dream I'd had one night of the garden dressed in moonlight. White as blue. Water as amber. The bravura of night birds.

Cocky

Weather is itself at Chanticleer. It falls where it will. Nothing but trees to poke up inside it. No industrial exhalations to mask its purpose. Maybe weather doesn't know its own power, but that doesn't negate its effect. Temperature. Cloud cover. Humidity. Wind. Rainfall. Either it blesses the ground and the green and the blossoms, or, out of stubbornness, it doesn't.

That day was perfect. Eighty degrees, blue, the half-moon at an uptilt in the sky. The breeze was constant, companionable, and gentle, and to the garden had come white-haired mothers and their graying daughters, fathers with little boys, gatherings of friends in fours and fives, an unusual number of cameras. The weather had put a cheer in us, and chattiness extended in all directions. A little girl by the pond was blowing soap through a plastic ring; "Look, look and see!" she pleaded with me (she had such huge black eyes), as she pointed to her bobbling and quite iridescent soap globes. A man and his friends were precariously concluding that the sorghum was maize and the silver willow trees were Russian olives, but then, because I was passing by, they solicited my opinion. "Sorghum," I said. "And willow trees," a half-guess and a challenge. Laughing, they crowned me an expert.

"We'll take a tour with her," they said to each other, for my benefit. "You will be our tour guide," they said to me.

"Come back," I told them. "Come back next week," and they turned and went on their way.

Up at the terrace, meanwhile, another man with another mane of white hair was feigning royalty as he stood at the balcony and looked out across the docile lawn. "All I need now," he told me as I passed, "is one good butler."

"A butler?" I said.

And he said, "A butler and an ice man, a chauffeur and a car. Not to mention a couple of answers. Is that a fig tree over there? Is that hydrangea?"

"Maybe," I said. "Probably," and he laughed and announced to the kingdom he now ruled, "Therein stands my fig tree!"

"That's where they keep their jewelry," said a little girl who ran to me.

"Their jewelry?" I asked, and she said, "Yes, yes," as she pointed to the apple house. I followed her down the hill a bit. The apple house was filled with dried flowers.

"You see?" she said.

"Um-hmmm," I said. "Can you tell me what kind of jewelry?"

"No," she said. "Tell me."

I could convince no one that I hardly knew a thing. No one wanted to hear it. No one wanted to relinquish the pleasure of conversation in that blue and gauzy theater. We were all trafficking in bits of news, no matter how slight or faux.

"If pumpkin comes from pumpkin seeds," a sweatered lady said to me, "then passion fruit must come directly from passion flower. That, in any case, is my new theory, and I'm sticking to it."

Never mind that a storm was on its way. Never mind that the weatherpeople had been warning us for days against the monster winds that the coming hurricane was packing, against the floods that would no doubt uproot the trees and turn the world into cubism. Never mind that we knew this weather would not last — that the pink heads of the anemone would soon be tossed like old love letters; that the gourds where small birds nest would soon be pitching, hurling; that the benign stream would finally show its angry, insatiable side.

Never mind that we knew what was coming. We chattered and cheered as we made our way through Chanticleer, blithe because the present weather contradicts all notions of tomorrow. We were there for the moment, in that garden right then, a little high on optimism and goddamned cocky as the moon.

The Only Chance We've Got

*I*n the aftermath of the storm, the mood was somber. At the edge of the Asian Woods it looked as if someone had taken a fine-toothed comb and yanked it through the California geraniums. In the stream lay shorn-off bits of trees. At the pond the lotus plants had all but dropped their sails, and the field of prairie drop seed had been flattened.

The talk among strangers and friends was quiet. The garden had been put in its place by weather, and so had the rest of us; we are so entirely miniscule in comparison to wind and rain and hail. We were aware of how everything was angled newly. Made jagged or raw. Thinned out. We were reminded of other storms that had blown in, then turned and vanished.

On that day only the gardeners seemed brave — hauling broken branches and clumps of errant leaves from wherever they had gotten to, straightening the stakes and invisible ties, suggesting, by the way they carried things, that the world could be made right again. The gardeners were muddy and burdened and resilient because love is the only chance a garden's got. For the moment, and in the moment. Now because of then.

What Every Grown-up Will Remember

One day at the vegetable garden a Korean woman was going on about a purple cotton plant. She wanted someone to come look, and so I stopped and did. I had seen her before, many times, this lady in her blue visor, and maybe she had seen me too, for she began to tell me stories, to trust me with them. About the garden at her church. About the granddaughter whose face she'd had silk-screened on her shirt. About the charms of Chanticleer, which was, she promised, the world's best pleasure garden.

We walked together, down the path, and she began to tell me tales of her Korea. Of how as a child she never went straight home from school but walked through fields and streams and collected crayfish and watched the cotton grow and bloom. Cotton is soft, white, sticky in the midst of its bloom, she confided. She'd break it apart and suck on it. She'd eat it going home.

When we got to the primary pond, this lady (much shorter than I, far more sure-footed) raised her hand in the direction of a batch of lovely flowers. These, she told me, were a meal in her Korea. As were a kind of lotus seed, as was the garlic grass.

"We'd make pancakes with the garlic grass," she said. "We'd eat lotus seeds like nuts. We'd eat the cotton; it was delicious. Oh, what you don't know about taste and gardens here."

I was distracted, in that instant, by a boy with a recorder who was playing like the pied piper. It was a white recorder that made a wispy la-de-da when blown into by this boy of no more than three. When the boy got right up to the edge of the pond he planted his feet and tossed his instrument into the air — theatrically leaned back and threw it. "I love it, I love it, I love it," he said, and just then two other boys emerged from a break in the woods, shouting, "Wow, wow, wow" to each other. I couldn't decide if the boys had come as friends or had accidentally happened on some shared adventure.

When I turned back toward my friend, I realized she was gone — that in the midst of wow and clamor she had disappeared. I looked both ways on the path and took a few steps back up the hill, until I heard but did not see her asking a gardener for purple cottonseeds. She would plant them at her church, she was saying. She would put them there so that they would tell a story about her childhood and God.

Out of sight, now, the boys were still playing. I could hear them at the water's edge, exclaiming over the turtles that swam between the lotus flowers. If only they could have one, they were saying, a single one, they'd take it home. They'd put it in a box and name it. They'd feed it insects from their yard. They'd do what every child does, and what every grown-up will remember.

Gifts

When it was time, the gardeners gave me seeds. I began to ask for them. The seeds themselves or the flowers that contained them. In buckets or hand to hand.

One gardener paddled out across the pond and returned with a gift of lotus — four petal-less stalks with sweet perforated pods, which I took home and tied a string around so that they might be hung beside a window.

Another gardener made a gift of something blue and bellish, and also pink and yellow begonia grandis. I was offered a big white fragrant flower — a datura, I was told (and wrote that down). And bits of butterfly weed and liverwort, euonymus and Chinese rain tree. I was greedy with the rain tree seeds and the leaves (like the finest Florentine paper) that

enclosed them. I took them home and filled a bowl, then arranged the rest on my sills.

I had no real plan to plant the seeds this time; I just wanted their companionship and beauty. I wanted to be able to turn from the work on my desk and see the promise, the *potential*, of seeds on a shelf, seeds in a jar, seeds in a bowl, seeds that rattled in the browned cups of their perforated pods. Seeds that had been given as (so many) gifts to me: Take this. Take this. Take that one.

"What are the seeds for?" my son asked me again.

And I said, "They are for what is already past. And they are for the future."

At This Hour of the Day

*T*hree ladies on a bench, their hair bright white. The beautiful, luminous, perfect white of a downy woodpecker's breast. One braids a few strands of grass in her hands, and one looks out, over the hill, through dark glasses, and one rests her head on the back of the bench and tilts her face up, toward the sun, taking its heat. I love the color of these ladies' hair, its unadorned, unpainted whiteness. I love the companionable nature of their easy, unaccusing silence. Stories have passed between them, I think, and stories have passed out of reach, and the air is cool, and the air is sweet, and the sun is where it climbs to, at this hour of the day.

Walk a circle, and they're sitting there. Walk it again, and they haven't moved. They are like flowers planted in the ground, flowers ripe with the end of season. A breeze might stir and take their seeds. Someone might come and kiss them.

Romance

It happened that I met the gardener who'd thought to nest the girl inside the pond. He had found her, he told me, near one of the houses, sitting in dry air, on a pedestal, and she had seemed lonely to him, in need of water.

So he conveyed her down the hill (this I imagine as a struggle) and placed her in that little pond, making sure she did not topple. At first, the gardener said, the girl suffered from a slight miscalculation, for she had been placed so close to the small pond's edge that children stroked her head too often. So one day the gardener moved the girl out further toward the pond's just slightly deeper center, again taking care so that she would not fall or topple.

I told the gardener that at times (on darker days) I called this girl the drowning girl; disappointed, he shook his head.

She was not drowning at all, he said; her life was neither violent nor tragic. She was peaceful, she was serene, and besides, she was in love with an old catfish. "Catfish?" I said, for I had seen the rosy-red minnows and the three goldfish and the uncountable frogs, but not a catfish. And he said, "A catfish, of course; he swam from far away to find her. Swam down a stream and up a pipe and through something else until he was there, where she was, with all those minnows.

"He's with her all the time," the gardener said. "And somehow you didn't see him."

The Part of You
That Loves Them

The day I took my husband to the garden it was hands-in-pockets weather. On the hill past the ruins, one of the gardeners was pulling last night's blankets from big ballooning flowers. On another hill, where Adolph's apple grove once stood, the limbs of crabapple trees were rimmed with bright red berries. By the terrace, the deeply dimensional passion flowers bloomed. All about, but especially near Adolph Senior's house, the leaves of the hydrangea were maroon.

They were letting things die at Chanticleer; such was the season. The skies were bright blue, but the air was cold, impatient, and my husband with his camera and I with my notebook were wishing we'd brought gloves. We walked together, side by side, and then we separated. I lost sight of him at the sorghum and wended my way down toward the woods.

There were few others about, owing to the wind, the cold, the season, and I wondered, as I walked alone, whether my husband would locate the garden's beauty. It was October, after all, and if you didn't know all the colors and all the songs that the garden had bloomed forth with, you might not be able to imagine or to gauge all that I'd come to need. I had told him and told him and told him about the garden, but my husband was walking in it now. Can you give away the things you love, or the part of you that loves them?

It was cold, and maybe it wasn't just the winds that were impatient. I hurried my pace and began to hunt for the man with whom I had arrived, the man with whom I've been for almost twenty years. It wasn't long before I found him (it never is at Chanticleer), but at first I kept my distance. For there he was, up on the terrace, appraising a passion flower with his camera. Stepping closer, stepping back, looking at it now from a new angle, and though he must have been cold (for it was very, very cold), he seemed content inside the picture. Happy to be where he was, happy to look at what I loved, happy to take my hand when at last I called his name.

We left the garden shortly after that and came back home, to seeds.

The Acorn and the Promise

*O*nce not very long ago I asked my husband who we will be when we grow up. When our son is really on his own and when the words are finally lifted from my desk and when the color has all but disappeared from our eyes, our hair, our skin: Who will we be then? How will we live, and how will we love? How will we see everything? I want to be tender when I grow up. I want to be wise, and believing. I want the child that I was to belong to me still, and I want creek mud on my feet and the throb of a frog inside my hand. And strawberries. I want that.

My husband said nothing, and nothing more was said, and thereafter I kept my questions to myself. My thoughts about ghosts and legacies, my dreams about moonlight on ponds. I'd go to the garden, and then I'd come home, measuring the distance between life and metaphor.

Weeks went by, and then one day I found a book on my desk. Not a book that I had written, but one my husband had. It was words and pictures. It was fantasy and fact. It was the acorn and the promise.

It was our world, transformed.

When We Grow Up

When we grow up
We will find a piece of land
Not too far but far enough.
And in time
(and bit by bit) we
Will build a house.
It will be small but comfortable.
The rooms will
be painted in
colors much
brighter than
they should
and they will be filled
with your books

and my scribbles.

I will make the house,

You will make the garden.

We will meet in the

Terrace

(and the courtyard).

On weekends and some holidays

We will pack our spices and our good wine.

We'll invite the people

That we like

And talk about the things we've done

Or the places that we've seen.

It will be like a

story you once

wrote

or like a picture

I once dreamed, and in the morning

you will wear all white

and study how the light attaches to a petal

after the rain.

Chanticleer: The Biography

*I*n 1884 a certain Ellwood Harvey, MD, described the land from which Chanticleer would spring as bucolic, "well-watered" territory:

> Almost every country house is supplied from a never-failing spring of pure, soft water, and nearly all the fields of every farm have running streams through them.
>
> ...The rapid flow of these streams and their numerous branches have cut deeply into the surface of the land, making it beautifully diversified by wood-crowned hills and fertile valleys and hill-sides. No one who has ever seen the charming scenery of this part of our State can exclude from the recollection of it the well-tilled farms, with their tastefully-planned homes,

capacious barns, fields of waving grain, and the herds of cows that supply milk and butter of the very best quality to the Philadelphia market. Here grow luxuriantly all the fruits, grains, grasses, and vegetables of the temperate zone.

Two centuries before, William Penn had walked and tallied this land. Before Penn there had been adventurers and freedom seekers of Dutch and Swedish descent (men with names like Captain Hendrickson and ships with names like *Restless*), and prefatory to all that were the Lenni-Lenapes, who (according to Penn) were straight backed and black eyed. The Lenapes used dried bird claws to catch the fish they ate and deer shoulder blades to hoe the land they seeded. They carried a spear over one shoulder and a pelt of woven fur over the other. They trusted women with the art of growing food and put their faith in the Corn Mother. The Lenapes lived in bark houses and brewed hospitable pots of soup, and when they felt in need of a little mindful clarity, they set off for the sweat houses at the edge of town (one for the women, one for the men), drank medicinal concoctions, and sweated until it was time to chill off by rolling around in the snow. They never killed for the sake of killing, the Lenapes, never stood among the trees and streams and said, "This land belongs to me."

And yet for blankets and scissors and kettles and pewter spoons, the Lenapes traded away the land they loved to a man who (all records suggest) was fond of the Indians he'd found on "his" land. He thought well of their generally unhurried relationship to the earth. He admired the organization of their towns, the civility of their politics, the design of their bark houses. He respected the nobility of their posture. He did not run the Lenapes out of town with terror. He fashioned treaties; they accepted.

Later, Penn's own progeny would manipulate the treaty terms and exacerbate an incipient rancor between the newcomers and the natives. Later the fabled green country Penn had in theory parceled off would become a haphazard quilt of wide and narrow and short and long plots, as families arrived in boats, disputed boundaries, renegotiated deeds, set up housekeeping beside former Indian cornfields, and began to argue about taxation and governance. There would be, from then on, a stretch of earth known as the Welsh Tract. There would be the sound of falling trees. Houses made of logs and then houses made of fieldstones. Blacksmiths making much of iron deposits, millers harnessing streams, farmers overseeing fields of grain, a romance with sycamore trees.

Places with names like Merion and Haverford, Radnor and Goshen, Tredyffrin and Uwchlan would come into being. More houses would replace the trees. There would be herds of

cows and hillocks of grass and a tannery and a couple country
stores and wagons rumbling down dirt highways and the rudi-
ments of a library, and this would become the bucolic land that
Dr. Harvey would admire.

But it wouldn't end there: No wedge of land is ever free of
more consumptive dreams. Even as Harvey was writing, the
Pennsylvania Railroad was chugging through, with its oil lamps
and hot coal stoves and a brand-new generation of people.
Even as he was celebrating fields of grain, there were summer
boarders bringing revelry from the city, old taverns throwing
all-night parties, men with names like Cassatt and Drexel
who were buying up the charm. They built luxury homes,
these men. They threw luxurious events. They took the train to
their jobs in the city every day, then proudly took it home.
To cleaner air and brighter birds and more accommodating
weather. To great, green stretches of emerald lawn and backyard astronomy.

In unreasonable fits of false nostalgia, I try to stop the history
here. Try to turn the house lights back on and let the credits
roll. Show over. Land still green. Occasional houses on the
hills beneath the shade of sycamores. Because already it isn't
the land as it was — it's been carved up, shaped, dammed,
plowed, seeded, redirected.

And yet: It was still graceful, gentle land. Still home to mid-night hayrides and morning hide-and-seek, to the lightning-rod man and to Charades, to the unimpeded sound of birds. Still fresh-air country — a getaway for the Philadelphians jammed into the urban grids drawn out by William Penn. You could board a train in a mecca of brick and smoke, perpendiculars and dust, and step out, an hour later, into the shade of old trees, the irregular land-scape of hillocks and green, the suburban estates of the wealthy. There was a Devon Inn not far down the road. Blooded cattle and vegetable farms. A horse show once a year each May. Operatic parties of the bold. The facts become myths after the protagonists are gone. If the land does not tell, it remembers.

But there is no curbing the wealthy's enthusiasm for para-dise. No stopping the multiplication of estates on the hills, no whispering into developers' ears that the very things one finds most charming in this scene are the things that are being aggressively diluted by so many real estate campaigns.

So the movie rolls, and George W. Childs appears on the screen. A magnanimous man, a truly good and civic-minded man, who has made his name as the proprietor of the scru-pulous *Public Ledger* and has built an estate in a Main Line town that's called Bryn Mawr. He throws parties that everybody goes to — generals and presidents' wives, writers and European nobility, his own news delivery boys, his few-and-far-between neighbors — and he's gotten an idea about a chunk of land down the road, a town he's calling Wayne. His idea, as it's been written, concerns "the founding of a village with perfect sanitary regulations, with broad avenues and streets, and with comfortable, attractive homes which should be within the reach of men enjoying comparatively small incomes."

But it's not just an idea, it is a verifiable program since, with the help of his friend, the financier Anthony Drexel, Childs has pooled half a million dollars, hired the best and most innovative sanitation engineer of the era, and started in on some six hundred homes or "cottages" that will be fabricated of stone and brick, roofed with slate, finished in "imitation of hard wood," offer hot and cold water, and be "papered in the latest style." You can buy one of these cottages "on easy terms," with $5,250, or, if your future's that much brighter, with $7,200. Or you can rent one, if that better suits your style. You can try this country living out, in other words, and you will never suffer boredom. Already there are famous Wayne hotels for summer boarders (billiard tables! liveries! wraparound porches for evening gossip!), a well-stocked Wayne drugstore, a Wayne bakery, a Wayne saloon, a Wayne opera house, and a Wayne lyceum. There are schools for your kids, improving rail conditions, and train conductors who are keen to learn your name, your needs, and your habits.

Roll the movie, just let it roll. For there's no putting a halt to the building boom that will accelerate as Childs's town

succeeds, pick up pace as the new century dawns, and go expo-
nential come 1914. Entire villages of Italian stonemasons will
be imported to work the fieldstone, carve out the pools, sink
and elevate the formal gardens. Some cattle reputedly worth
the price of diamonds will stand on the hills. A memory — or
is it envy? — of all things British will infiltrate the landscape.
And in 1913 into this mecca will come a family, the Rosengartens, whose money originates from a thriving chemical con-
cern and who are known, far and wide, as decent people.

It is the Rosengarten legacy that is preserved at Chanticleer. The thirty-some acres and the fence that protects them,
the private garden now open to anyone for the smallest fee, was
bought with Rosengarten money, loved with Rosengarten
hearts, preserved for all eternity by a bold Rosengarten will.
The land that is now a pleasure garden was, as we have seen,
at first the Rosengarten estate. A multigenerational compound
that became its own Magna Carta. Chanticleer is the hill, the
splinter of stream, the green that a Rosengarten rescued from
the incessant gnawing and buzz of development. It is the line
that got drawn because enough is enough. Because someone finally had to stop the madness and give the land some room to
breathe.

They'd come from the city, the Rosengartens, buying seven
acres of land from a farmer named John Bell, joining other

members of the extended Rosengarten family in the fashion-able migration to the country. Adolph Senior had been in the family chemical business since 1892 (quinine, it had all begun with quinine), and he was its secretary and treasurer when it merged with another chemical giant in 1905. The new firm was Powers-Weightman-Rosengarten Co., manufacturing chemists for the pharmaceutical trade, and in twenty-two years, through the complicated maneuver of a second merger, PWR would become Merck & Co., the largest pharmaceutical manufacturer in the country.

Adolph Senior had wealth and privilege; certainly, that's obvious. But Adolph Senior had vision, too; he wasn't dull in the way money can make one dull; he had a sense of humor. Over the course of his lifetime, he would midwife the University of Pennsylvania's Mask and Wig Club, co-write a history of a scientific institute, serve in Puerto Rico during the Spanish-American War, sit on the War Industries Board, and mastermind two additional houses for the Chanticleer estate. The first would be annexed to the property in time for Adolph Senior's son, Adolph, to move in with his new wife. The second would be built from the ground up for the daughter, Emily, who would become a bride a few years later.

But the true hero of this tale, as we know, is Adolph Junior, the boy who would evolve into the man who spent most

of his adult life conspiring to preserve the land that he profoundly loved. Because he had grown up there. Because he had
taken a dogcart to nearby towns for ball games or to do carpen-
try. Because he had clambered up trees, come home muddy,
helped with the Victory Garden during the war years, cele-
brated the branching out of apple trees. Because he had walked
a mile and a half to church on Sundays and on the weekdays
had gone off to school in a steam locomotive that encrusted
him with cinders in hot weather.

Adolph had dreamed of being a landscape architect, but
the family urged him to become a lawyer. He had met a woman
who was taller than he and taken her home to the house his
father had built. He had a penchant for all things British, had
famous novelist friends, took hunting trips to England, and
had his share of worldly adventures, but Chanticleer was his
home; he had walked its hills most every day. Gone up and
down. Eaten its fruit. Listened for its birdsong. He had considered the earth and the value of the earth; he had said how much
he loved it: "You can go around for miles and miles, through
many countries, but you won't find as attractive rolling country
with the incredibly beautiful trees that we have here."

There are the ghosts of what has been. There are the ghosts
of what never was. Adolph, who had no children of his own,
grew up and grew older, witnessed encroachments, began to

despair at the graying of the green: There are so many consumptive dreams. It was the 1960s, it was the 1970s, and all
about Adolph the farms were coming down and the cows were
shipping out and the color of the sky was growing less trans-
parent. All about him were subdivisions and suburban malls,
congested roads and vanquished trees.

Which is, in the end, the point of all this telling. Which is
where this history ends and where this history also begins:
Adolph, the boy who did become a lawyer, the man who once
went undercover as a spy, the man who hoped to go down in
history as a landscape gardener, went down instead as a philan-
thropist. There was no other choice, the way he once ex-
plained it. There was nothing else to do:

> Since it is such beautiful countryside, really, with the
> folds of the ground, the streams, the lovely trees, I'm
> very worried it will not be preserved; sooner or later it
> will be all split up into developments and small houses
> and that means shopping centers. So what my wife and
> I propose to do is to maintain this place as a center, the
> Chanticleer Foundation, for the education of people
> who are coming out here from the city who don't
> know anything about trees or shrubs or flowers. It will
> be a little bit of open space, perhaps, but primarily to

help these people landscape and keep their places beautiful and attractive. . . . People who move out from town don't know that if you put a Norway Spruce in front of a picture window it won't be long before it's all shade and no view. It's not altogether despairing, perhaps, if we can see that places aren't too small and see that people who do come out learn to love the ground, love the smell of the countryside.

Adolph would not leave the world despairing. He'd leave it Chanticleer. Leave his land in the hands of gardeners and of the rest of us who love the soil and the seeds.

Sources

PREFACE

"Sometimes we seem to smell of decay..." Karel Čapek, *The Gardener's Year*, Michael Pollan, series ed. (New York: Modern Library Gardening, 2002), 107.

"poetry worn away as if by acid..." Pablo Neruda, in Luis Poirot, *Pablo Neruda: Absence and Presence*, Alastair Reid, trans. (New York: Norton, 1990), 38.

A TALENT FOR LIVING

"Keenly observed, the world is transformed..." Gretel Ehrlich, *The Solace of Open Spaces* (New York: Penguin Books, 1985), 7.

PRESENT TENSE

"At a given place..." John McPhee, *In Suspect Terrain* (New York: Farrar, Straus and Giroux, 1983), 65.

OPTIMISM

"lovers, farmers, and artists..." Gretel Ehrlich, *The Solace of Open Spaces* (New York: Penguin Books, 1985), 84.

GREEN FOR US

"In every thing that nature makes..." Louis Kahn, in John Lobell, *Between Silence and Light: Spirit in the Architecture of Louis I. Kahn* (Boulder, CO: Shambhala, 1979), 12.

RIDING THE BREEZE

The relationship between the age of the dinosaur and the dawn of flowers is noted in Loren Eiseley, *The Star Thrower* (New York: Harcourt Brace, 1978), 66–75.

ANOTHER WAY OF SEEING

"All changes, even the most longed for..." Anatole France, frequently quoted aphorism.

CHANTICLEER: THE BIOGRAPHY

"Almost every country house..." Ellwood Harvey, in *History of Delaware County, Pennsylvania*, Harry Graham Ashmead, ed. (Philadelphia: L. H. Everts, 1884), 1.

"the founding of a village..." The information about George Childs and the founding of Wayne was drawn from the various reprinted newspaper articles and personality sketches assembled in Harvey, *History of Delaware County*, 1.

"You can go around for miles..." Adolph Rosengarten, interview with Jean La Rouche, November 1978 (audiocassette).

"Since it is such beautiful countryside..." Adolph Rosengarten, interview with Jean La Rouche, November 1978 (audiocassette).

For information on the history of the Main Line, I turned to the following sources: Winifred B. Alterbury, ed., *Radnor: A Pictorial History* (Wayne, PA: Suburban and Wayne Times, 1992); Ashmead, *History of Delaware County;* J. W. Townsend, *The Old Main Line* (n.p.: PA, 1922); the good people and assorted documents and artifacts of the Radnor Historical Society; and the profound expertise of Jeff Groff, Executive Director of the Wyck Association.

For information about the Lenni-Lenape Indians, I turned to the following sources: William Cornell and Millard Altland, *Our Pennsylvania Heritage* (Harrisburg, PA: Penns Alley, 1983); Paul A. W. Wallace, *Indians in Pennsylvania* (Harrisburg, PA: Pennsylvania Historical and Museum Commission, 1999); and John McPhee, *In Suspect Terrain* (New York: Farrar, Straus and Giroux, 1983), 65.

For information about Chanticleer and the Rosengarten family, I turned to these sources: Lorett Treese, *The Rosengartens and Chanticleer* (Wayne, PA: Chanticleer, 2000); the audiocassette interview of Adolph Rosengarten conducted by Jean La Rouche in November 1978, held by the Radnor Memorial Library; and, mostly, the reminiscences of Howard Holden and Marilyn Caltabiano.

Recommended Reading

*S*ometimes, when it rains or when the garden gates are closed, I turn to the books on my shelves and escape into other writers' dreams of cloudscapes and roses, other writers' love of landscape, earth, and place. Among those books are the following:

Burnett, Frances Hodgson. *The Secret Garden* (a novel)

Čapek, Karel. *The Gardener's Year*

Cobbett, William. *The American Gardener*

DeBlieu, Jan. *Wind: How the Flow of Air Has Shaped Life, Myth, and the Land*

Dillard, Annie. *Pilgrim at Tinker Creek*

Ehrlich, Gretel. *The Solace of Open Spaces*

Elliott, Brent. *Flora: An Illustrated History of the Garden Flower*

Gordon, Mary. *Seeing Through Places: Reflections on Geography and Identity*

Halpern, Sue. *Four Wings and a Prayer: Caught in the Mystery of the Monarch Butterfly*

Hamblyn, Richard. *The Invention of Clouds: How an Amateur Meteorologist Forged the Language of the Skies*

Heinrich, Bernd. *The Trees in My Forest*

Hinchman, Hannah. *A Trail Through Leaves: The Journal as a Path to Place*

Hobhouse, Penelope. *The Story of Gardening*

Hogan, Linda, and Brenda Peterson. *The Sweet Breathing of Plants: Women Writing on the Green World*

Hubbell, Sue. *A Country Year: Living the Questions*

Humphreys, Helen. *The Lost Garden: A Novel*

Kingsolver, Barbara. *Small Wonder: Essays*

Klinkenborg, Verlyn. *The Rural Life*

Logan, William Bryant. *Dirt: The Ecstatic Skin of the Earth*

Mitchell, Henry. *One Man's Garden* and *The Essential Earthman*

Montgomery, Sy. *The Wild Out Your Window: Exploring Nature Near at Hand*

Ondaatje, Michael. *Running in the Family*

Pavord, Anna. *The Tulip: The Story of a Flower That Has Made Men Mad*

Perenyi, Eleanor. *Green Thoughts: A Writer in the Garden*

Pollan, Michael. *The Botany of Desire: A Plant's-Eye View of the World* and *Second Nature: A Gardener's Education*

Rember, John. *Traplines: Coming Home to Sawtooth Valley*

Russell, Sharman Apt. *Anatomy of a Rose: Exploring the Secret Life of Flowers*

Sarton, May. *Plant Dreaming Deep*

Tompkins, Peter, and Christopher Bird. *The Secret Life of Plants*

Warner, Charles Dudley. *My Summer in a Garden*

Willard, Pat. *Secrets of Saffron: The Vagabond Life of the World's Most Seductive Spice*

Williams, Terry Tempest. *Refuge: An Unnatural History of Family and Place*

Wright, Richardson. *The Gardener's Bed-Book: Short and Long Pieces to Be Read in Bed by Those Who Love Green Growing Things*

Acknowledgments

As the Executive Director of Chanticleer, Bill Thomas has opened the gates of the garden to me on every imaginable occasion. He has encouraged this book, believed in it, and insisted on nothing but that the prose be true to my perceptions of a place he sensed I loved. For his good humor and friendship along the way, I am grateful.

My long-time agent, Amy Rennert, and her colleague Dena Fischer read this book the day it arrived at their office and immediately (and with great grace) embraced it; they didn't rest until they'd found an editor who would love it as they had. For their faith and friendship (and for a jubilant call made late one Thursday night), I am indebted.

At New World Library, Georgia Hughes has been an extraordinary advocate for *Ghosts in the Garden*, a generous editor, and a burst of deeply welcome kindness. I extend thanks as well to Kristen Cashman for the wise suggestions that contributed so

profoundly to the final shape and look of this book, to Mimi
Kusch for spectacularly graceful copyediting, to Mary Ann Casler
for the lovely cover and text design, and to Tona Pearce Myers for
making the words sit just right on the page.

Many have interrupted their plans to sit or stand or walk
with me, speaking of the garden. I wish to thank Howard
Holden, the formerly "long-haired" gardener, for a memorable
walk on a bright, cold day and for the subsequent conversations and encouragement; I owe some of my favorite parts of
this book to him. I wish to thank as well Marilyn Caltabiano,
the former head of the Radnor Memorial Library, who made
her way to the garden in the wake of a terrific storm just to
share (at my request) her recollections of Adolph Junior and
Chanticleer. I wish to thank Jeff Groff, who is, among other
things, the Main Line's resident historian and who provided
me with insights (and reading suggestions) with what I am
supposing is characteristic generosity. I wish to thank Christopher Woods, the "British horticulturist" and former executive
director of Chanticleer, who brought so much ingenuity, passion, and imagination to the garden and who shared stories of
its making. I wish to thank the Chanticleer board for its support of this admittedly quirky project by a serial garden-goer.
And I must, of course, thank the gardeners and staff of Chanticleer — in particular Laura Aiken, Dan Benarcik, Doug

Croft, Joe Henderson, Ed Hincken, Heather Klein, Dorothy Kunzig, Douglas Randolph, Lisa Roper, Laurel Voran, Prze-mek Walczak, and Jonathan Wright — who patiently answered my questions, broadened my vision, and sent me home with buckets of seeds and stalks of lotus. The seeds are still here. The lotus hangs from a string near the window.

Finally, deep appreciation to Ivy Goodman, who read this book before any other, brought her magnificent intelligence to it, and (throughout a long, cold winter) believed. To Sy Montgomery, who uses the word *exquisite* just when a woman needs to hear it. To Jennie Nash, Rahna Reiko Rizzuto, and Alyson Hagy, who listened. To Susan Straight and her daughter Rosette, for the jar of seeds and the sleeve of larkspur, the box of irises, and the many conversations. To Terry McElfresh Downes, for her contagious mettle and persevering enthusiasm. To my mother, Lore Kephart, for the countless blooms she has carried into my life or had delivered to my doorstep. To Jeremy, who loves the garden for his own quite perfect reasons. And to my husband, Bill, who came to understand and honor my passion for Chanticleer, who wrote the perfect poem, and who has stood in the rain and snow and sun to photograph the garden in all its many moods.

About the Author
and
About the Photographer

*B*eth Kephart is the author of a memoir trilogy and of *Seeing Past Z: Nurturing the Imagination in a Fast-Forward World*. Her first book, *A Slant of Sun: One Child's Courage*, was a National Book Award finalist and Salon.com winner; her second, *Into the Tangle of Friendship: A Memoir of the Things That Matter*, was written with the support of an NEA grant. Frequently anthologized, Kephart's essays have appeared in the *New York Times*, the *Washington Post*, the *Chicago Tribune*, Salon.com, *Real Simple*, *Organic Style*, *Lifetime*, *Redbook*, and elsewhere. She lives in a Philadelphia suburb with her husband, William Sulit, and their son, Jeremy.

*W*illiam Sulit is a Yale-educated architect, illustrator, and photographer. This is his first book.

New World Library is dedicated to
publishing books and audio products
that inspire and challenge us to improve
the quality of our lives and our world.

Our products are available
in bookstores everywhere.
For our catalog, please contact:

New World Library
14 Pamaron Way
Novato, California 94949

Phone: (415) 884-2100 or (800) 972-6657
Catalog requests: Ext. 50
Orders: Ext. 52
Fax: (415) 884-2199

E-mail: escort@newworldlibrary.com
Website: www.newworldlibrary.com